PIANO • VOCAL • GUITAR

BILLY JOEL TURNSTILES

Additional editing and transcription
by David Rosenthal

ISBN 978-1-4768-1668-5

7777 W. BLUEMOUND RD. P.O. BOX 13819 MILWAUKEE, WI 53213

In Australia Contact:
Hal Leonard Australia Pty. Ltd.
4 Lentara Court
Cheltenham, Victoria, 3192 Australia
Email: ausadmin@halleonard.com.au

Visit Hal Leonard Online at
www.halleonard.com

Peter Cunningham 1976

Turnstiles was Billy's third album on Columbia Records, his fourth album as a solo artist. Released in May of 1976, *Turnstiles* was a transitional work that celebrated Billy's move from California back to his home state of New York. He said good-bye to Hollywood, and began the New York state of mind that would inspire him for years to come.

Having played keyboards in Billy Joel's band since 1993, I have become very familiar with his music. In 2008, Billy asked that I review the sheet music to his entire catalog of songs. As I am also a pianist, he entrusted me with the task of correcting and re-transcribing each piece, to ensure that the printed music represents his songs exactly as they were written and recorded.

The challenge with each folio in Billy's catalog is to find musical ways that combine his piano parts and vocal melodies into playable piano arrangements. First, the signature piano parts were transcribed and notated exactly as Billy played them on the original album (i.e. the classic intros to "New York State of Mind" and "Miami 2017," the majestic "I've Loved These Days," and of course the fiery and energetic intro to "Prelude/Angry Young Man," etc.). The vocal melodies were then transcribed and incorporated into the piano part in a way that preserves the original character of each song.

Many people ask how to play the famous opening to "Prelude/Angry Young Man." The rapid 16ths on middle C should be thought of like a drum roll (in fact the part was originally inspired by the drum solos in the song "Wipe Out"). This part should be played leading with the right hand thumb and alternating with the left hand index finger. I've notated this accordingly by dividing the middle C's appropriately between the two staves. The right hand then makes the jumps to play the ascending thirds.

The intro and ending to "Miami 2017" are exactly as Billy played them. Since the ending fades out on the original recording, I included an alternate ending that is exactly how we perform it live. The classic "New York State of Mind" has an optional shorter ending, and although the complete intro is written out, I also indicated where to start if you'd like to begin with a simpler four-bar intro.

All of the arpeggiated piano parts in "Summer, Highland Falls" are written out exactly as Billy played them, but in the verses the part is modified to also include the vocal melody.

On "James," the two simultaneous Rhodes piano parts you hear on the record have been combined into a single playable part, and the flourishes that Billy plays between the vocal phrases are all intact. Even the sax solo is integrated into the piano part.

All of the songs in this collection received the same astute attention to detail. The result is sheet music that is both accurate and enjoyable to play, and that remains true to the original performances.

Billy and I are pleased to present the revised and now accurate sheet music to the album *Turnstiles*.

Enjoy,

David Rosenthal
March 2013

SAY GOODBYE TO HOLLYWOOD

Words and Music by
BILLY JOEL

Moderate Rock 'n' roll

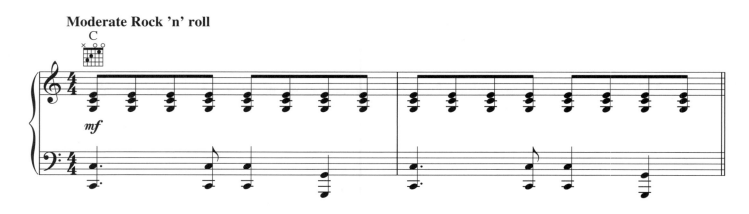

Bob - by's driv - in' through the cit - y to - night ____ through the lights ____
John - ny's tak - in' care of things for a while ____ and his style ____

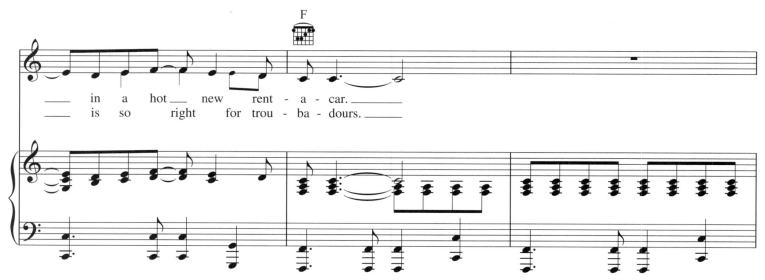

____ in a hot ____ new rent - a - car. ____
____ is so right for trou - ba - dours. ____

say a word out of line

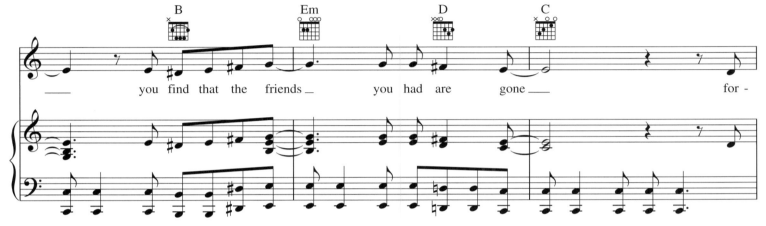

you find that the friends you had are gone for -

ev - er for - ev -

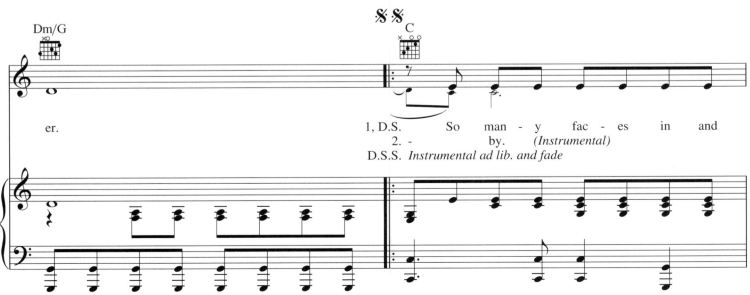

er.

1, D.S. So man - y fac - es in and
2. - by. (Instrumental)
D.S.S. Instrumental ad lib. and fade

out of my life ____ some will last ____ some will just ____ be now ____

____ and then. ____ Life is a ser-ies of hel-

los and good-byes ____ I'm a-fraid ____ it's time for good-bye ____

____ a-gain. Say good-bye to Hol-ly-wood,

say good-bye, my ba - by; say good-bye to Hol -

ly - wood, say good-bye, my ba -

(End instrumental)

say good-bye, my

ba - by.

David Ghar Studio

SUMMER, HIGHLAND FALLS

Words and Music by
BILLY JOEL

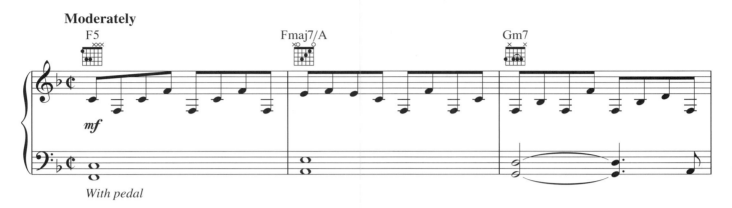

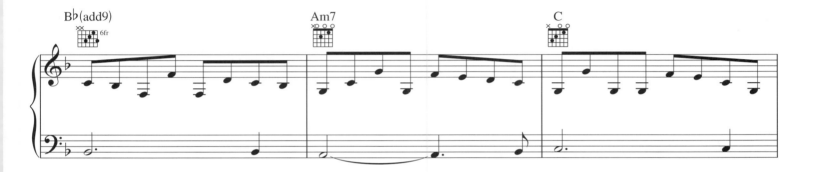

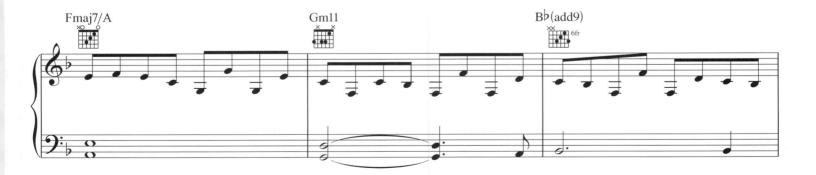

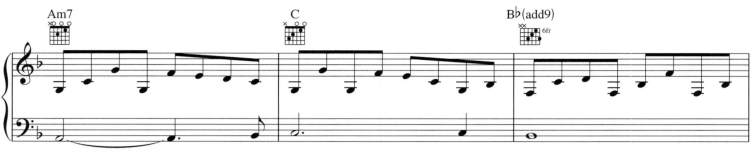

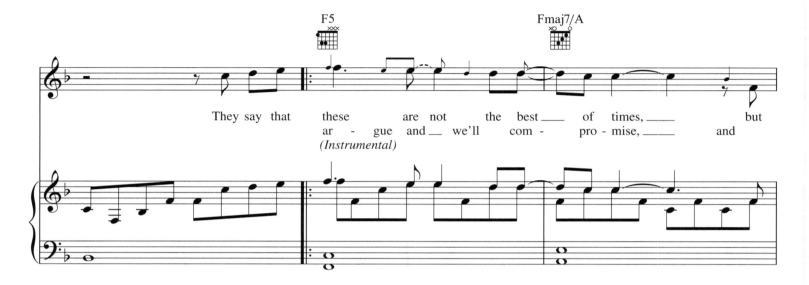

They say that these are not the best ___ of times, ___ but
ar - gue and ___ we'll com - pro - mise, ___ and
(Instrumental)

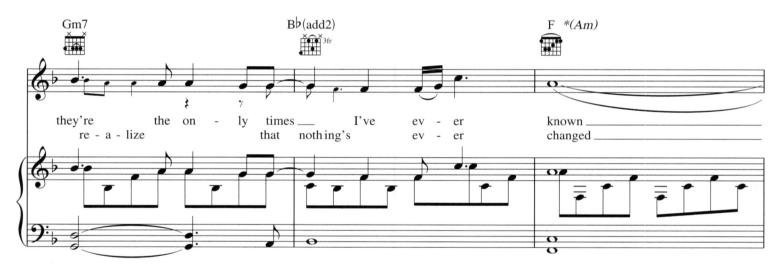

they're the on - ly times ___ I've ev - er known ___
re - a - lize that noth - ing's ev - er changed ___

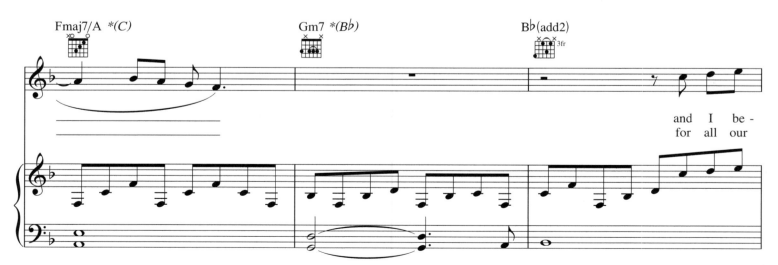

and I be -
for all our

These alternate chords are played during the Instrumental section only. For the piano accompaniment to these 3 measures, look to measures 5–7 on the first page.

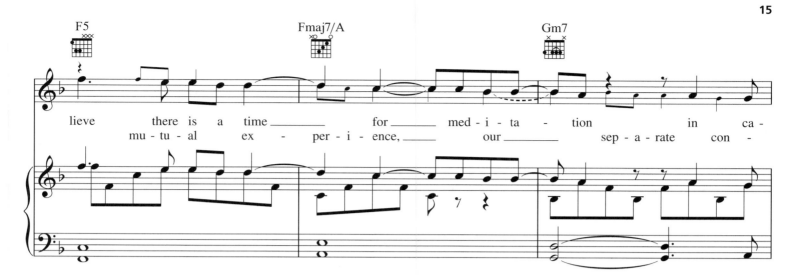

lieve there is a time _____ for _____ med-i-ta - tion in ca-
mu-tu-al ex - per-i - ence, _____ our _____ sep-a-rate con -

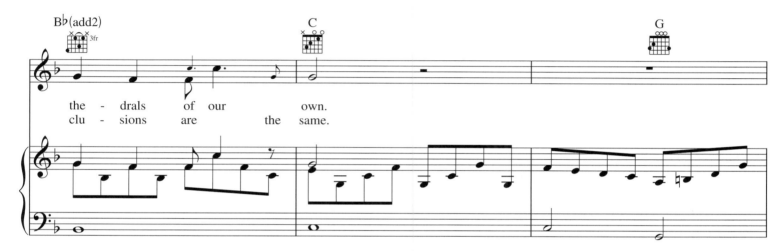

the - drals of our own.
clu - sions are the same.

(End instrumental)

Now I have seen that sad sur-

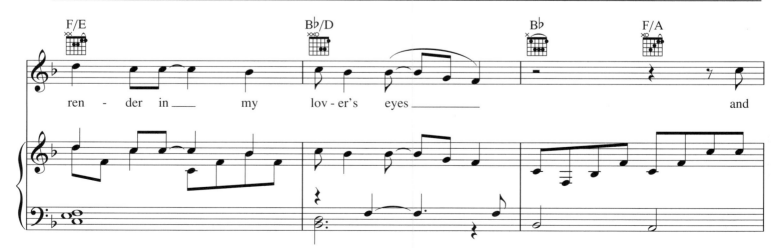

ren - der in _____ my lov-er's eyes _____ and

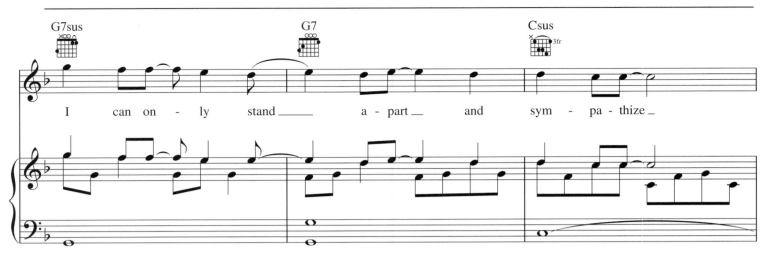

I can on - ly stand ____ a - part ____ and sym - pa - thize ____

For we are al - ways what our sit - u - a - tions hand ____

____ us, it's ei - ther sad - ness or ____ eu - pho - ri - a.

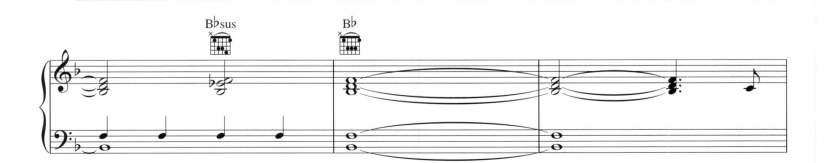

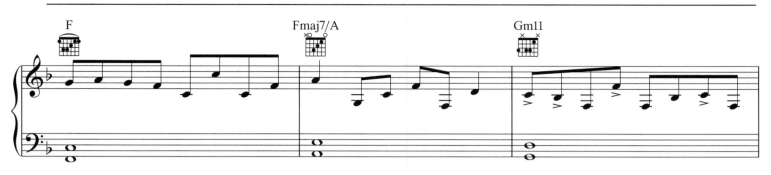

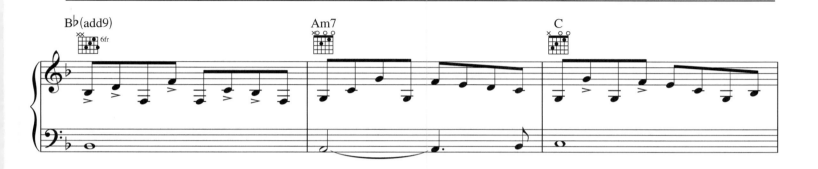

So we'll Now we are

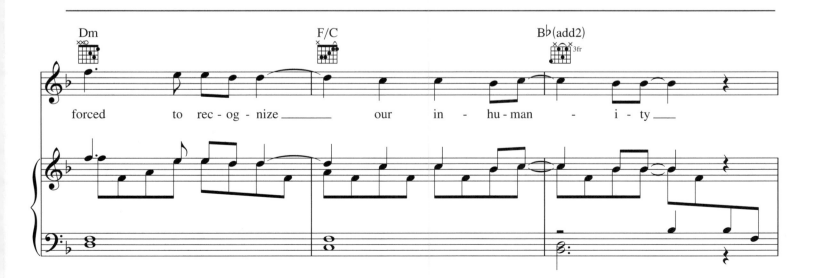

forced   to rec - og - nize _____ our in - hu - man - i - ty ___

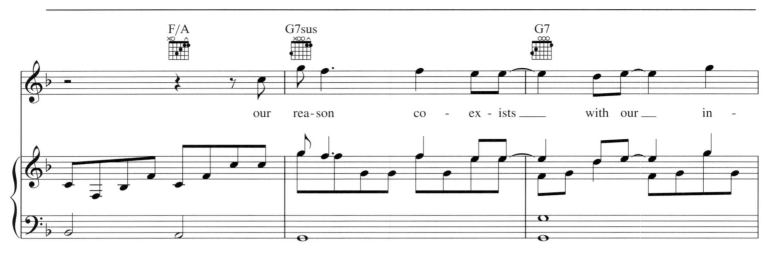

our rea-son co- ex- ists _____ with our _____ in -

san - i - ty _____ And though we choose be- tween re- al -

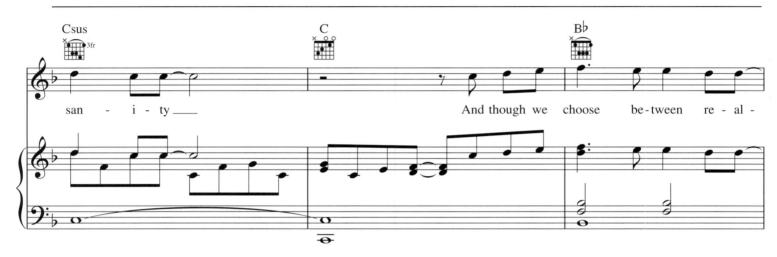

- i - ty _____ and mad - ness it's ei - ther sad - ness or _____

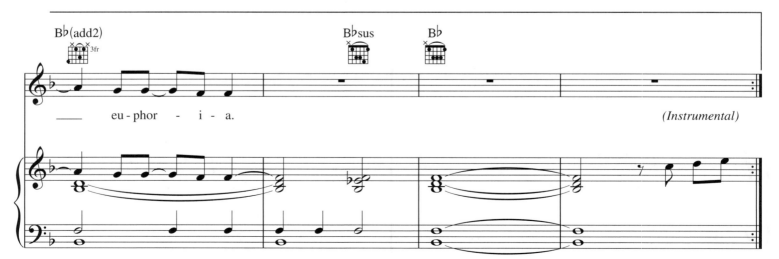

_____ eu - phor - i - a.

(Instrumental)

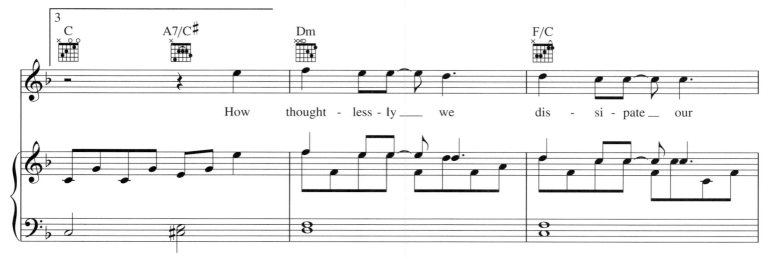

How thought - less - ly ___ we dis - si - pate ___ our

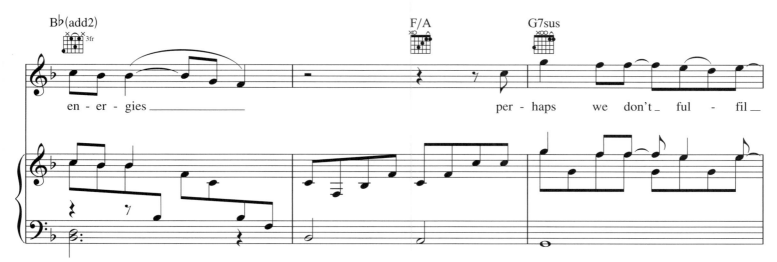

en - er - gies ___ per - haps we don't ___ ful - fil ___

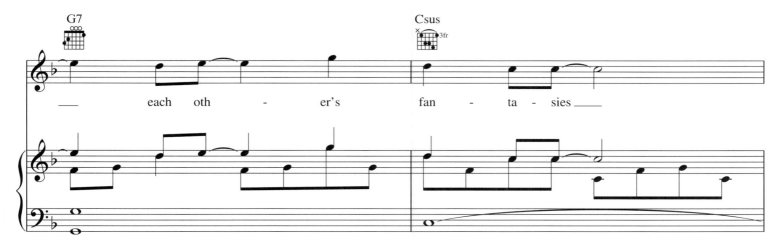

___ each oth - er's fan - ta - sies ___

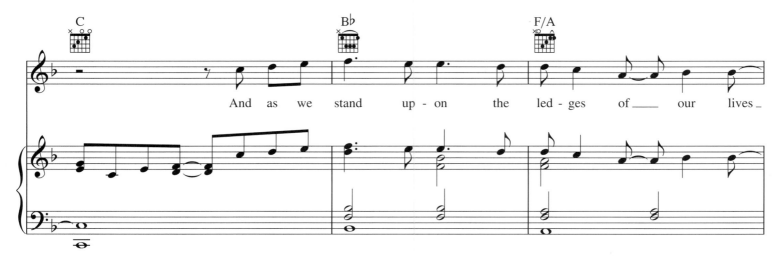

And as we stand up - on the led - ges of ___ our lives ___

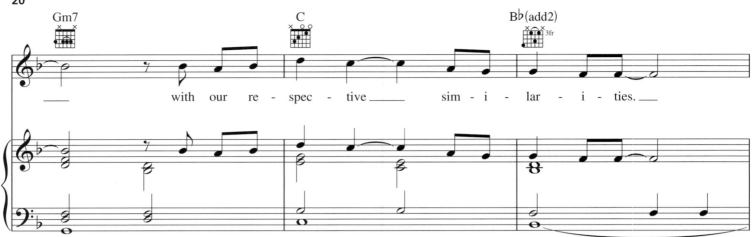

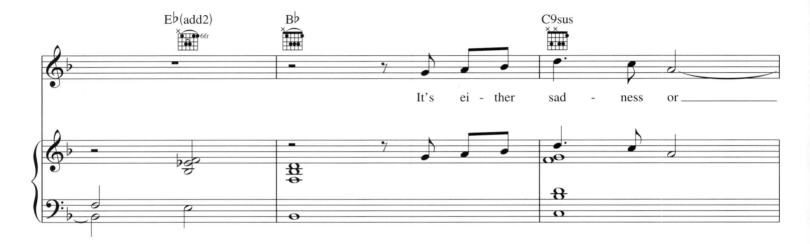

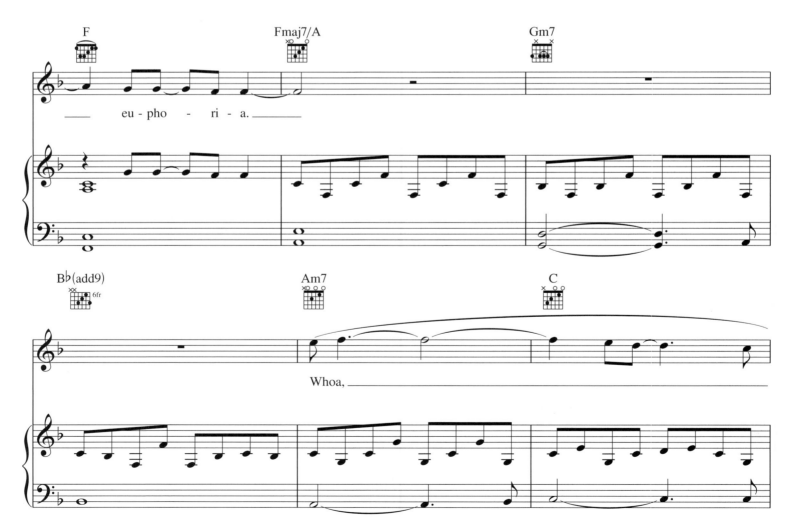

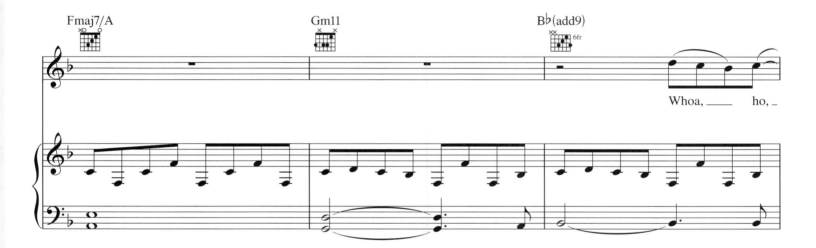

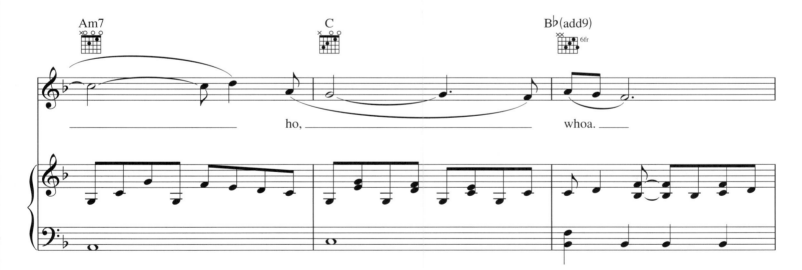

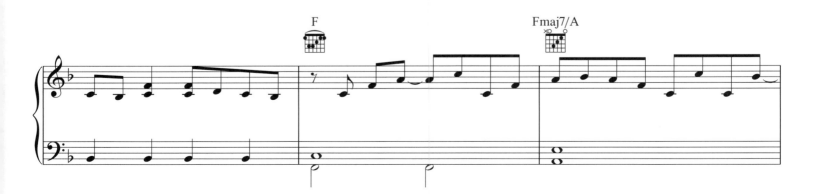

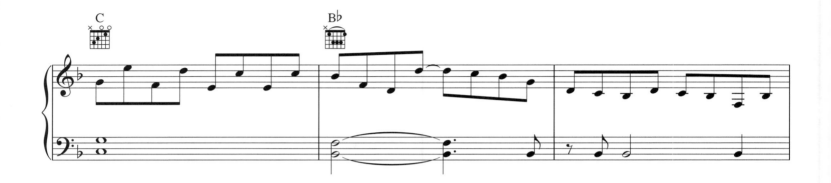

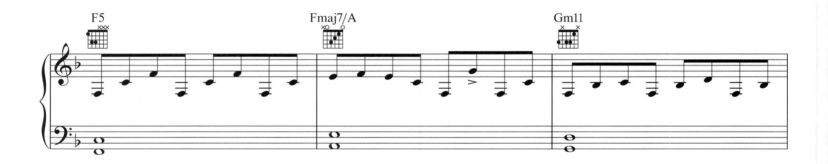

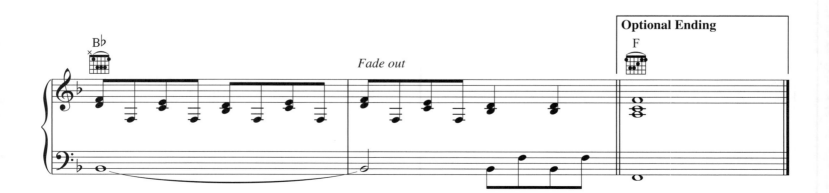

Caribou Ranch, a recording studio built in a converted barn in the Rocky Mountains near Nederland, Colorado. Turnstiles was completed here.

ALL YOU WANNA DO IS DANCE

Words and Music by
BILLY JOEL

Medium Reggae beat

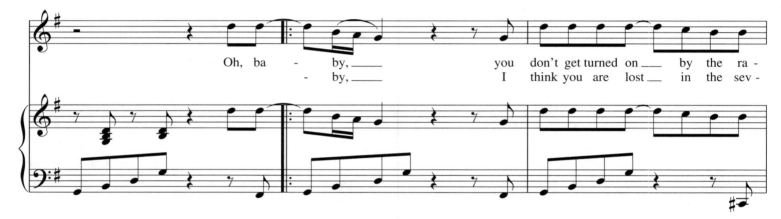

Oh, ba - by, _____ you don't get turned on _____ by the ra -
- by, _____ I think you are lost _____ in the sev -

di - o. Oh, ba - by, _____ you got
en - ties. Oh, ba - by, _____ the

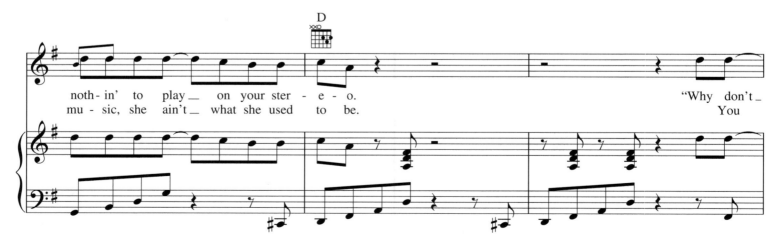

noth - in' to play _____ on your ster - e - o. "Why don't _____
mu - sic, she ain't _____ what she used to be. You

the Beat - les get back to - geth - er? Why don't
don't un - der - stand ___ what they're say - ing.

no - bod - y sing ___ of ro - mance? ___ Oh, ba - by, _____ all ___
Giv - in' it ev - 'ry ___ chance. ___

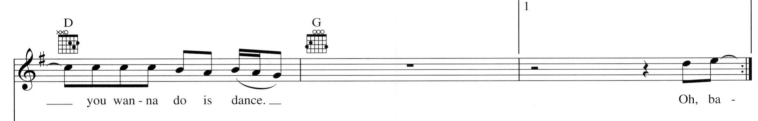

1

___ you wan - na do is dance. ___ Oh, ba -

2

Well, you wish you were back ___ in the good old days ___ when to -

ma - toes were cheap - er. _____ And you nev - er heard the words of your

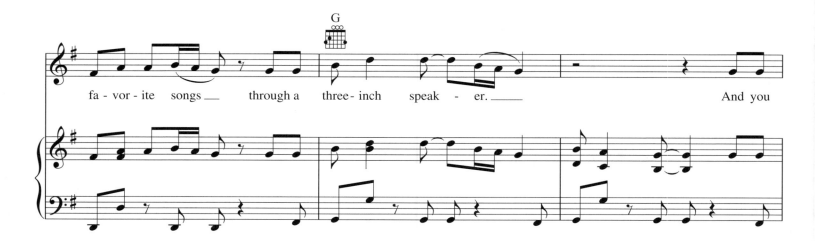

fa - vor - ite songs _____ through a three - inch speak - er. _____ And you

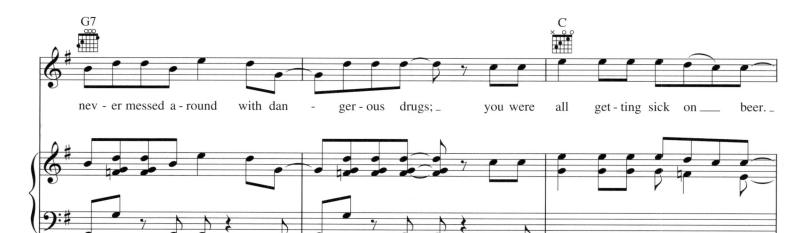

nev - er messed a - round with dan - ger - ous drugs; _____ you were all get - ting sick on _____ beer. _____

_____ And you did - n't get an - y un - less _____ you went stead - y and made

out for a year. _

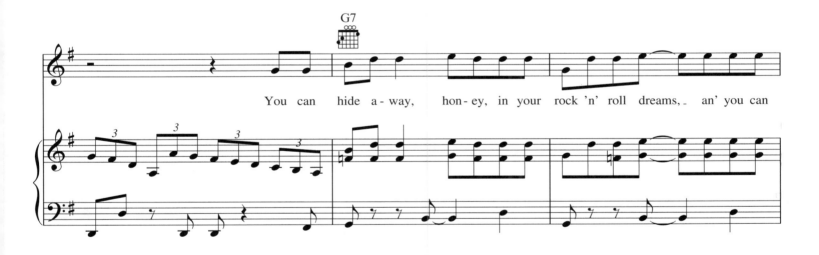

You can hide a-way, hon-ey, in your rock 'n' roll dreams, _ an' you can

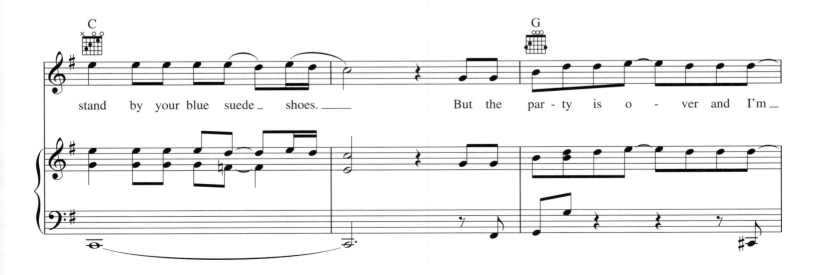

stand by your blue suede_ shoes. _____ But the par-ty is o-ver and I'm_

__ get - ting ti - red of wait - ing for you. __ Oh, ba -

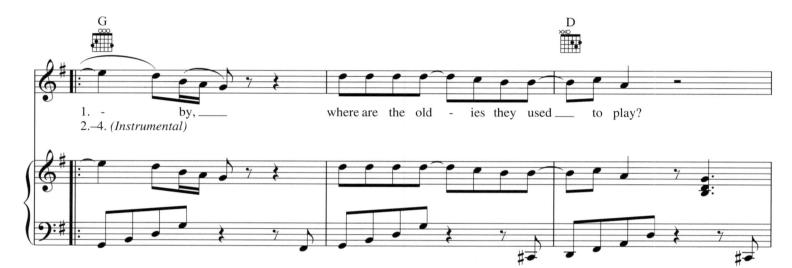

1. _ by, __ where are the old - ies they used __ to play?

2.–4. *(Instrumental)*

Oh, ba - by, __ you want to crawl back in - to yes - ter - day. __

You don't want to deal __ with the fu - ture. You

don't want to make an-y plans. _____ Oh, ba - by, _____ all _____

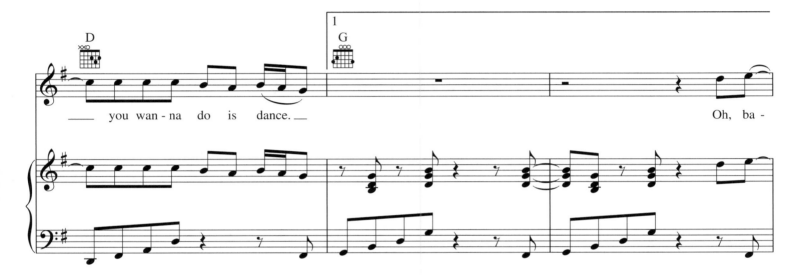

_____ you wan-na do is dance. _____ Oh, ba -

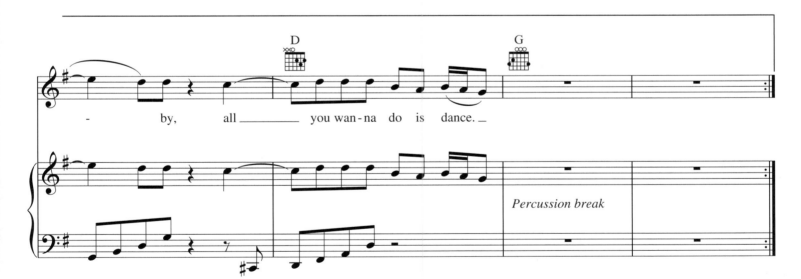

- by, all _____ you wan-na do is dance. _____

Percussion break

Repeat for instrumental verse and Fade

Percussion break

NEW YORK STATE OF MIND

Words and Music by
BILLY JOEL

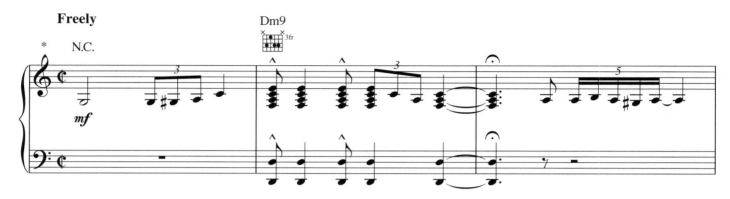

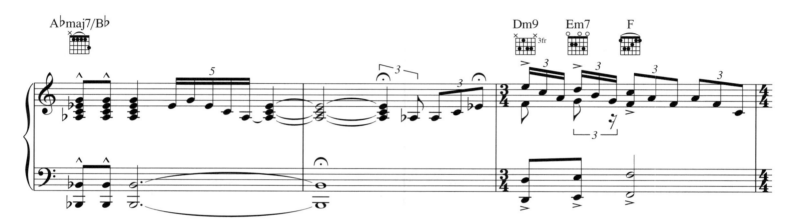

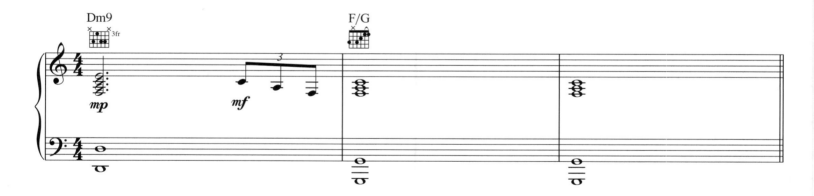

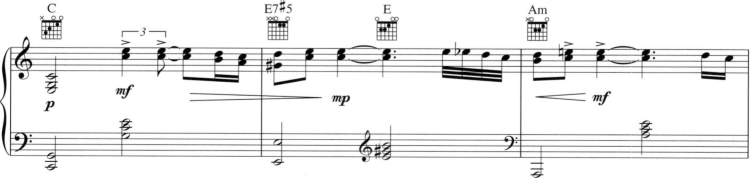

A shorter option for the introduction is marked on the next page.

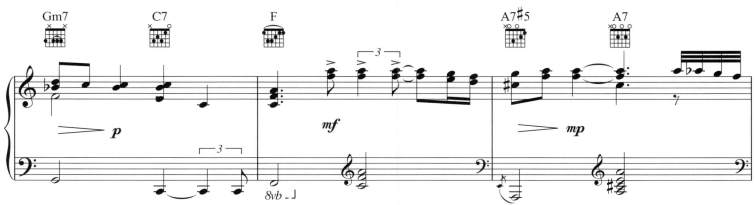

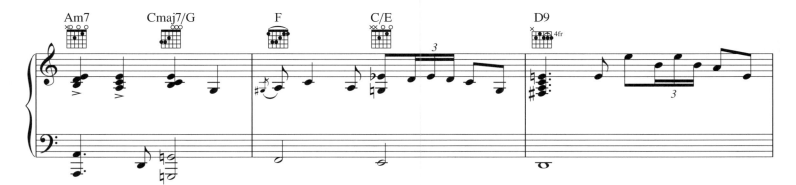

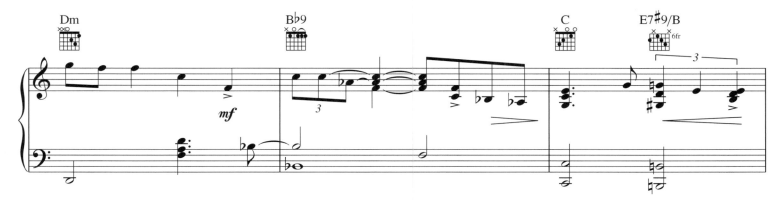

(Optional shorter intro)

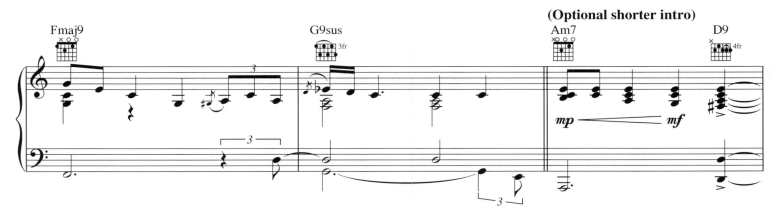

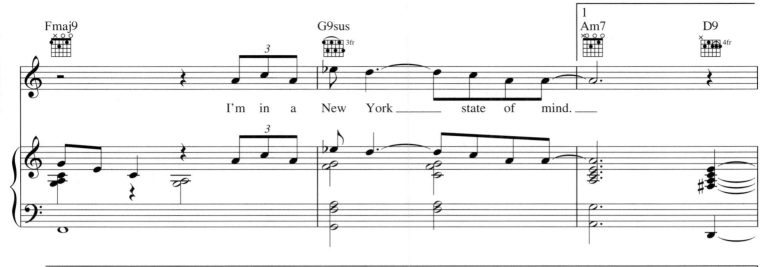

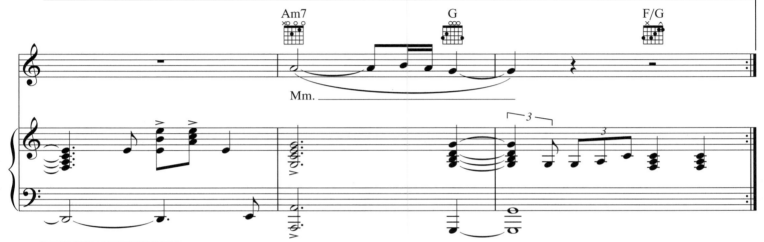

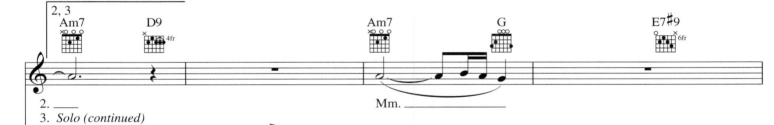

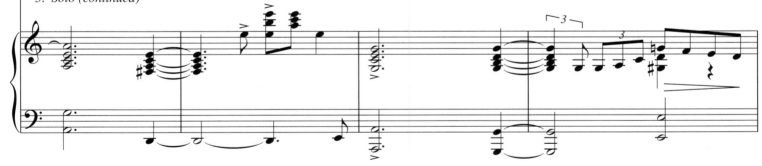

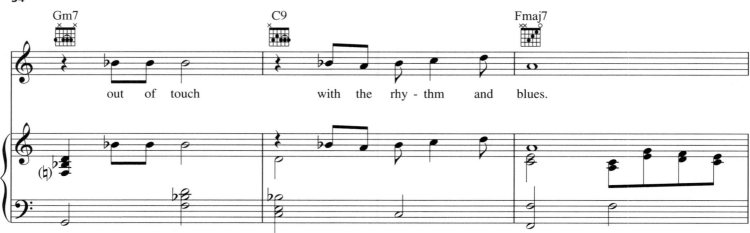

out of touch   with the rhy - thm and blues.

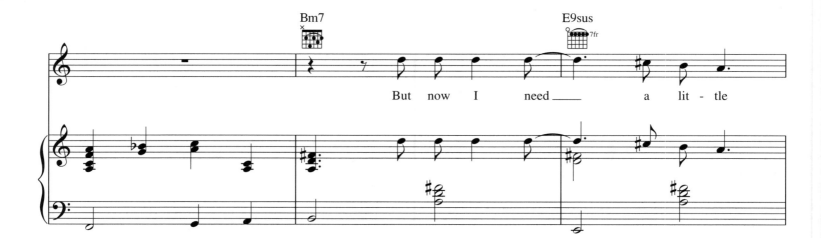

But now I need _____ a lit - tle

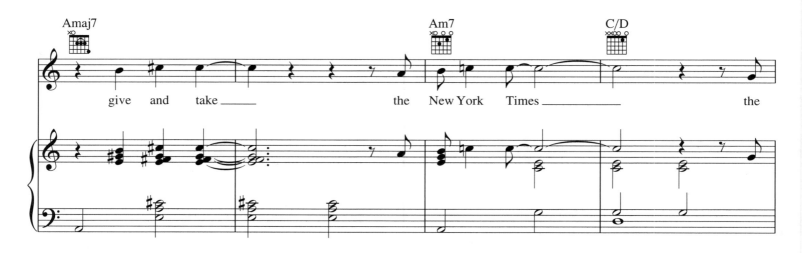

give and take _____ the New York Times _____ the

Dai - ly News. _____

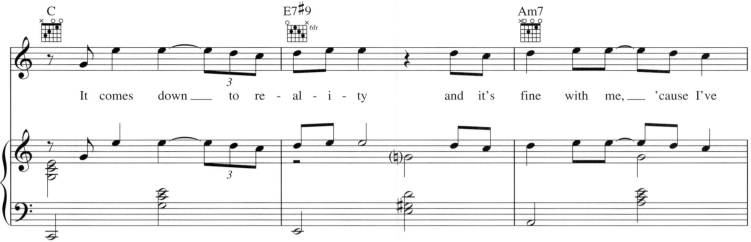

It comes down ___ to re-al-i-ty and it's fine with me, ___ 'cause I've

let it slide. Don't care ___ if it's Chi-na-town or on

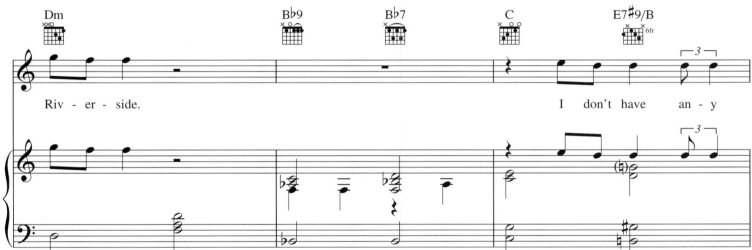

Riv-er-side. I don't have an-y

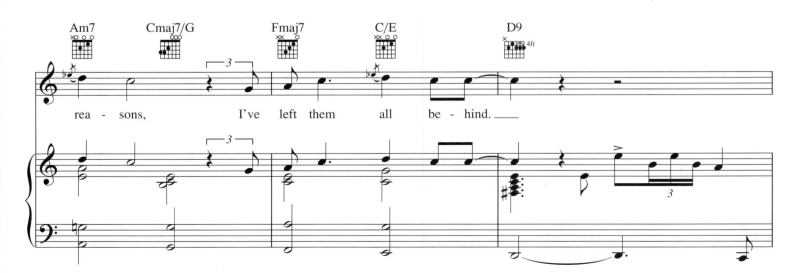

rea-sons, I've left them all be-hind. ___

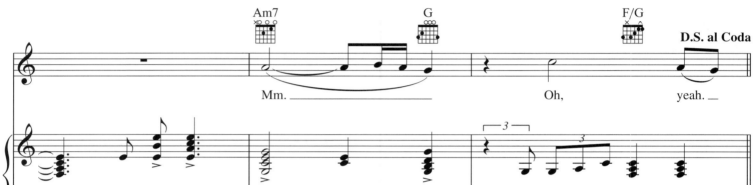

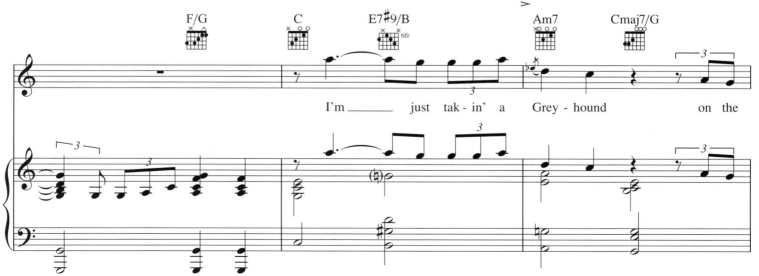

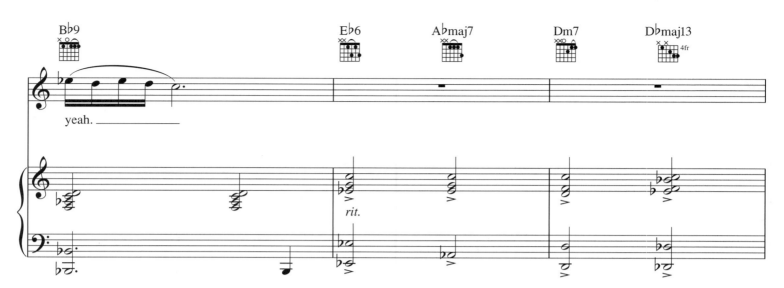

Optional short ending

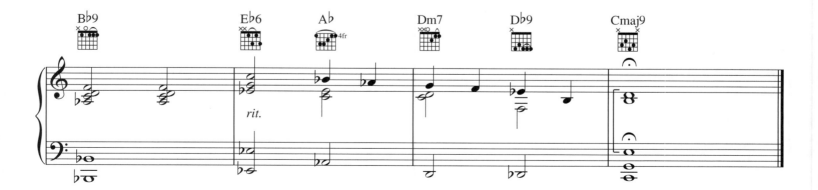

Turnstiles Tour Program Cover 1976

JAMES

Words and Music by
BILLY JOEL

Slowly, in 2

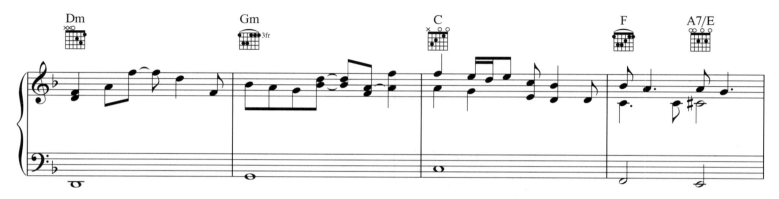

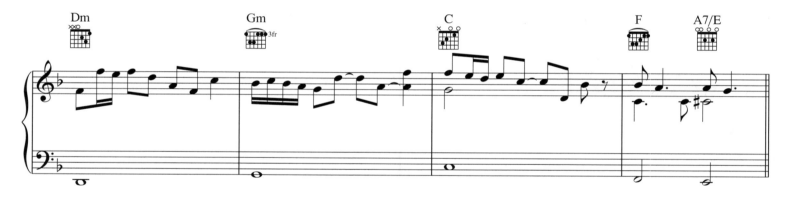

James
James

We were al-ways   friends ___
Do you like your life _____

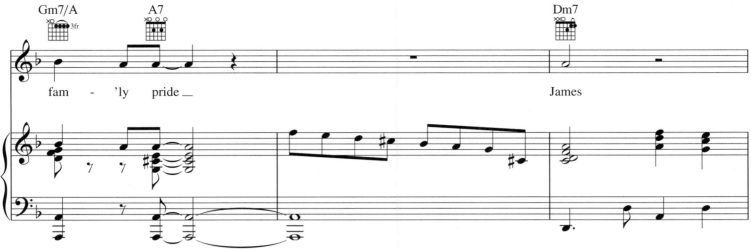

fam - 'ly pride ___   James

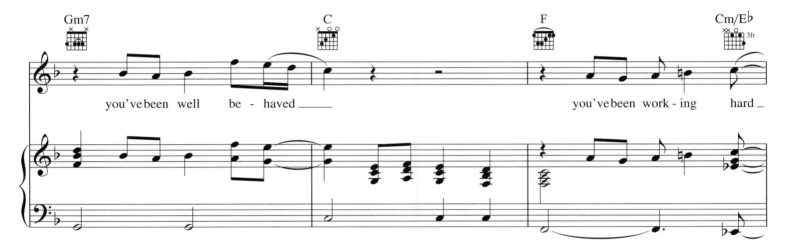

you've been well be - haved ___   you've been work - ing hard _

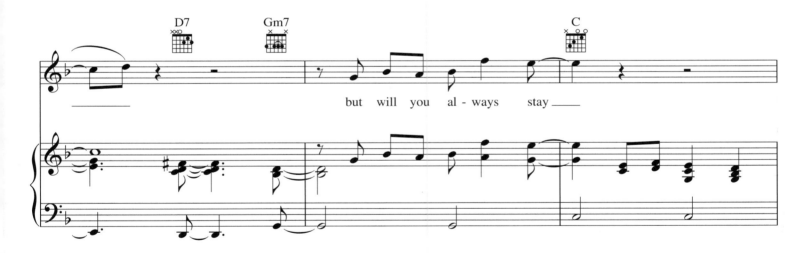

but will you al - ways stay ___

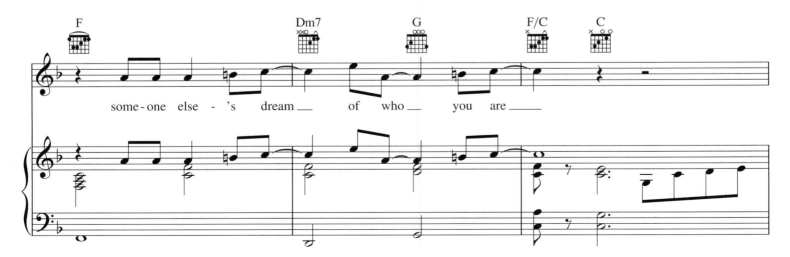

some - one else - 's dream ___ of who ___ you are ___

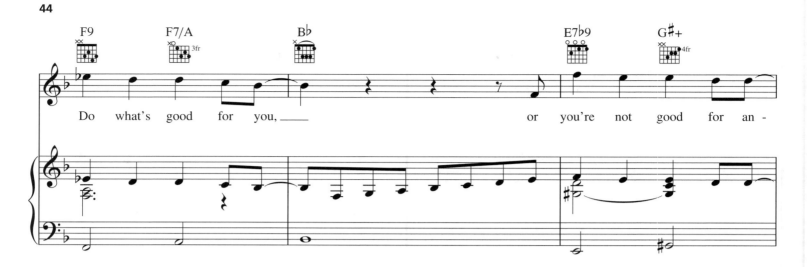

Do what's good for you, _____ or you're not good for an -

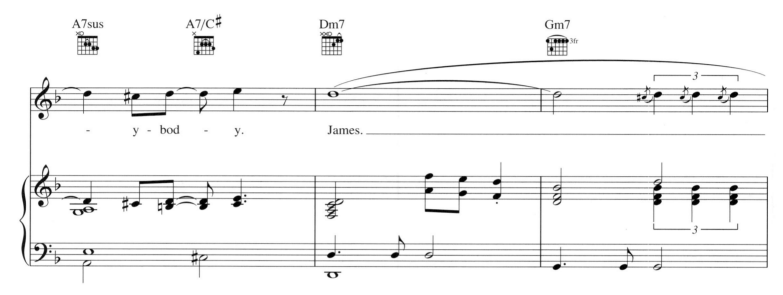

- y - bod - y. James. _____

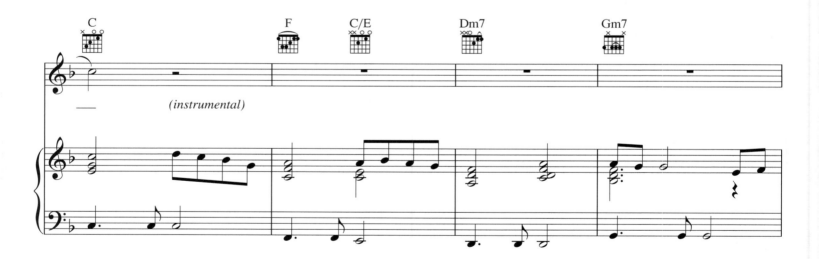

(instrumental)

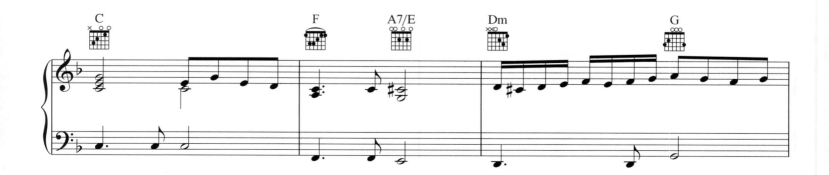

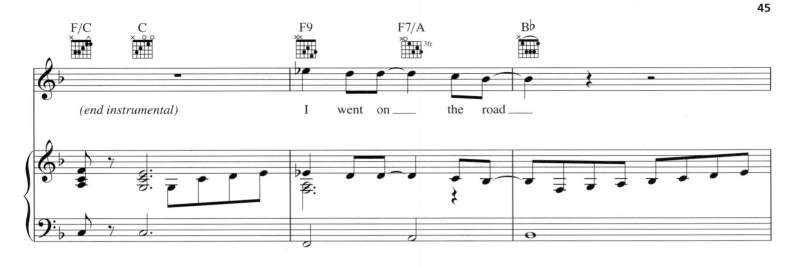

(end instrumental)

I went on ___ the road ___

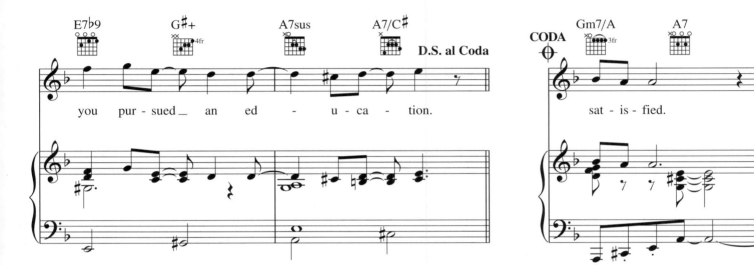

you pur-sued ___ an ed-u-ca-tion.

D.S. al Coda

CODA

sat-is-fied.

James

do you like your life? ___

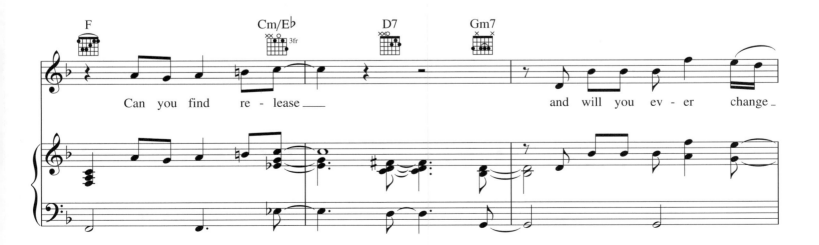

Can you find re-lease ___

and will you ev-er change ___

when will ___ you write ___ your mas - ter - piece? ___

Do what's good for you, ___ or you're ___

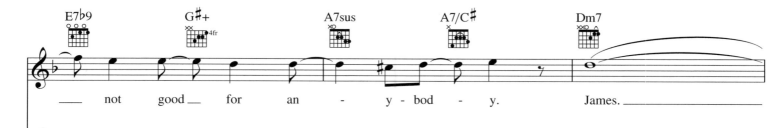

___ not good ___ for an - y - bod - y. James. ___

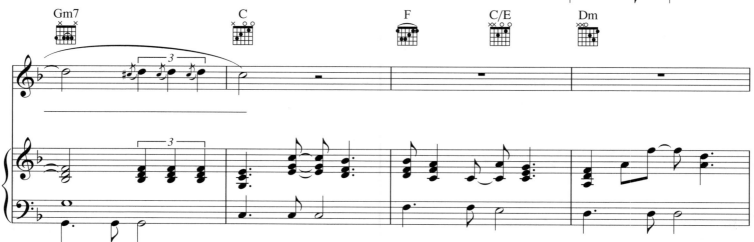

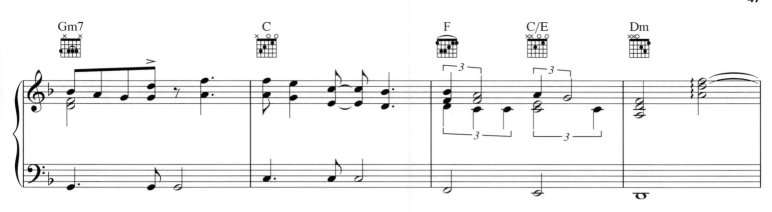

Live 1977

PRELUDE/ANGRY YOUNG MAN

PRELUDE
By BILLY JOEL

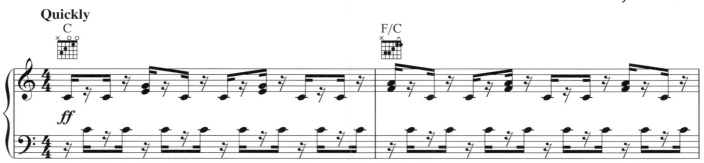

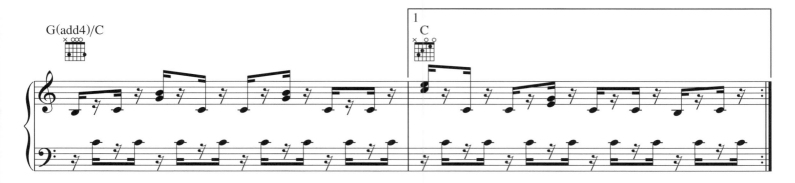

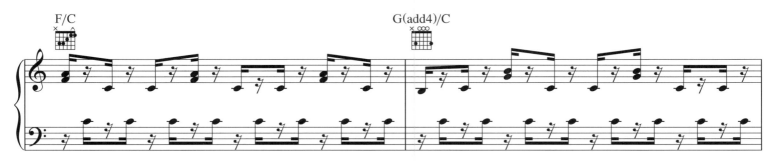

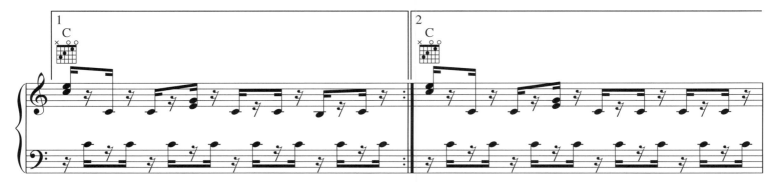

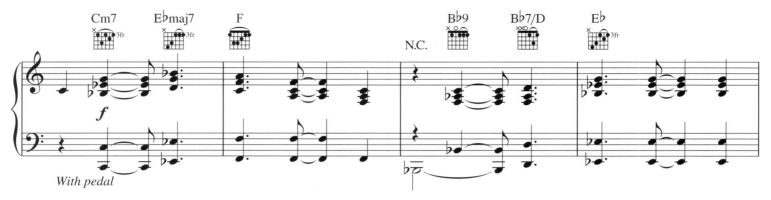

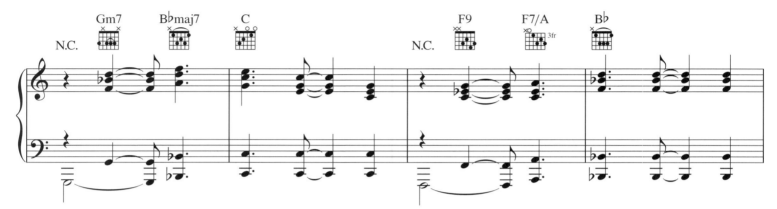

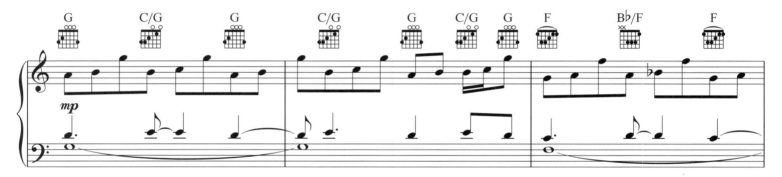

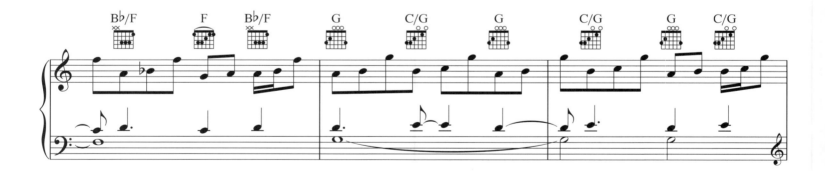

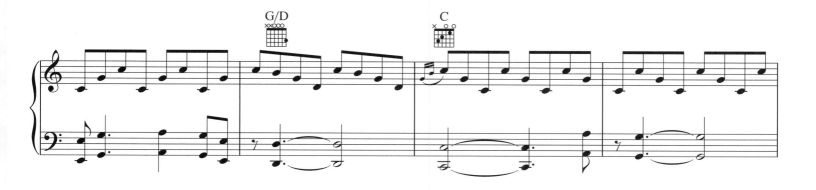

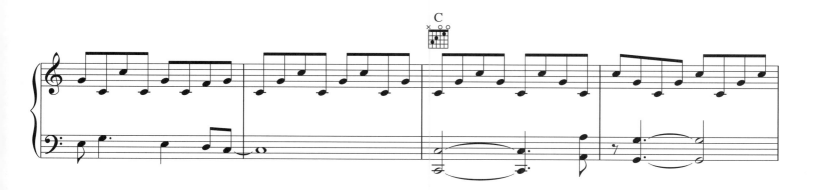

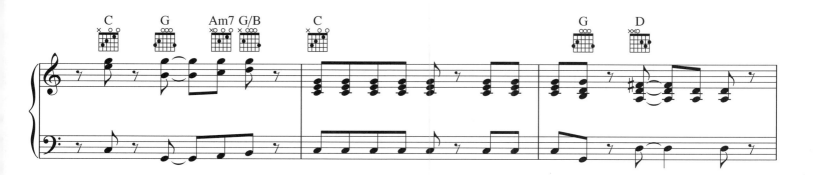

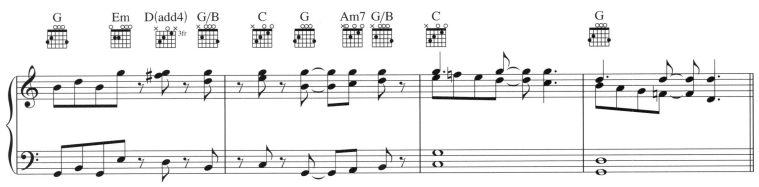

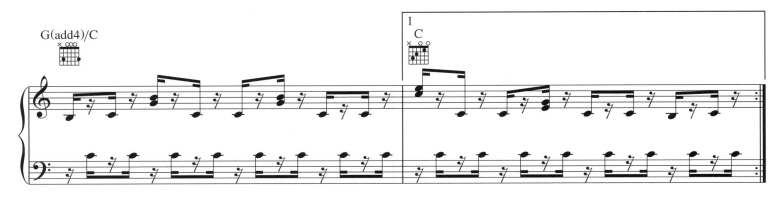

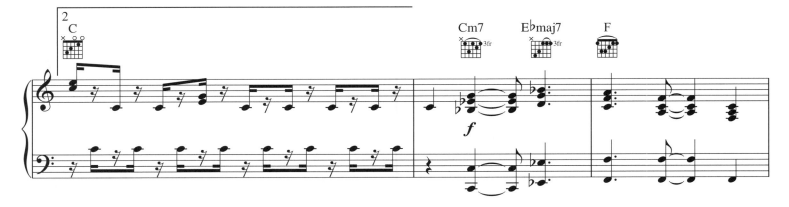

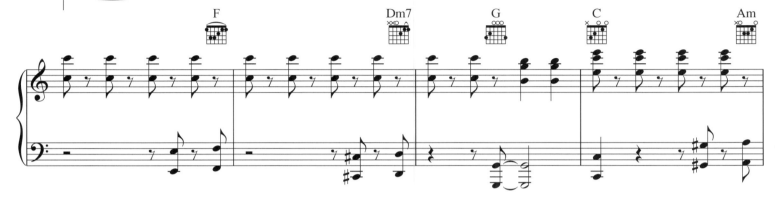

ANGRY YOUNG MAN
Words and Music by BILLY JOEL

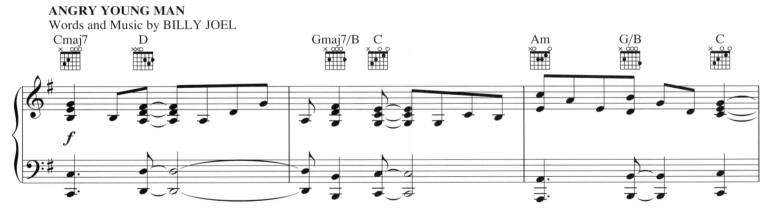

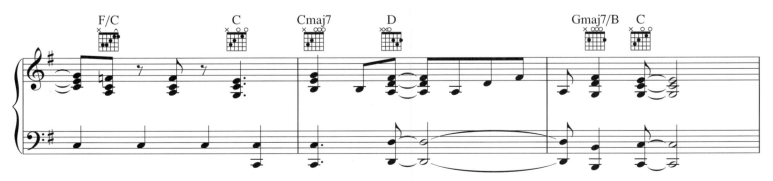

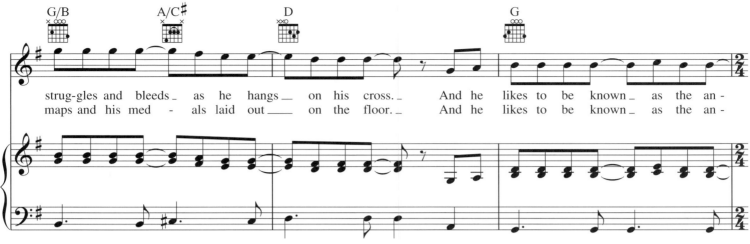

struggles and bleeds_ as he hangs_ on his cross._ And he likes to be known_ as the an-
maps and his med - als laid out___ on the floor._ And he likes to be known_ as the an-

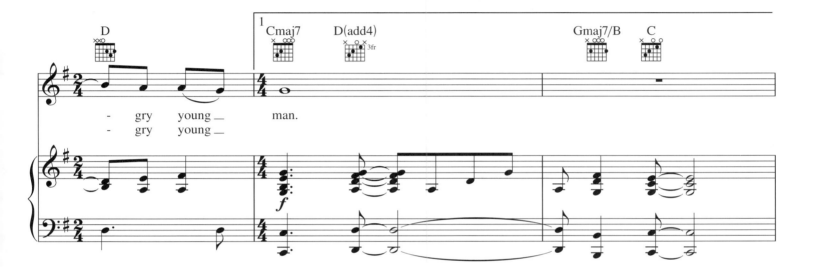

- gry young _ man.
- gry young _

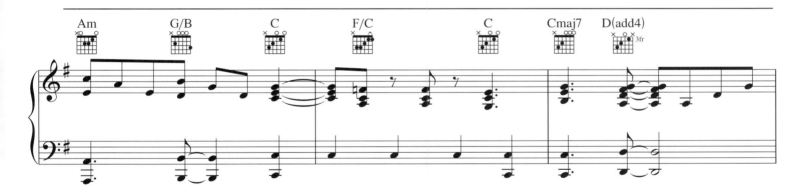

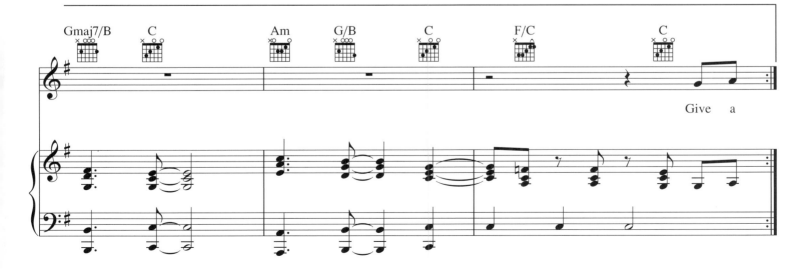

Give a

man.

1. I be-lieve I've passed the age ___ of
2. (Instrumental)

con - scious - ness ___ and right - eous rage. I found that just sur - viv -

- ing was a no - ble fight. ___

I once be - lieved in caus - es, too. ___ I had my point - less

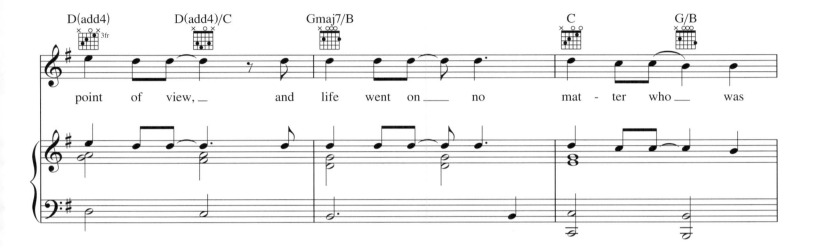

point of view, ___ and life went on ___ no mat - ter who ___ was

wrong or right. Oh. _____

___ *(end instrumental)*

But there's al - ways a place ___ for the an - gry young man with his
Yes, there's al - ways a place ___ for the an - gry young man with his

mp

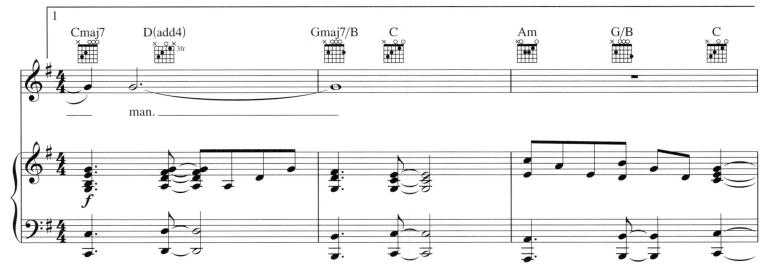

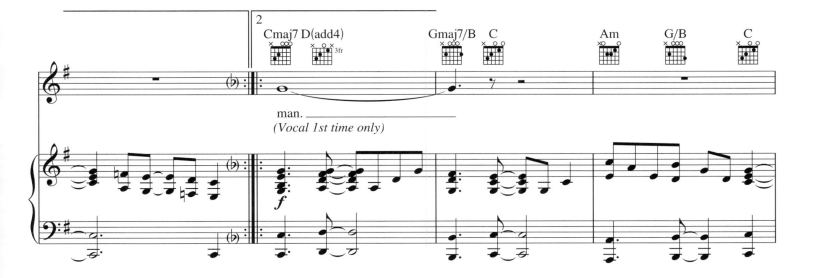

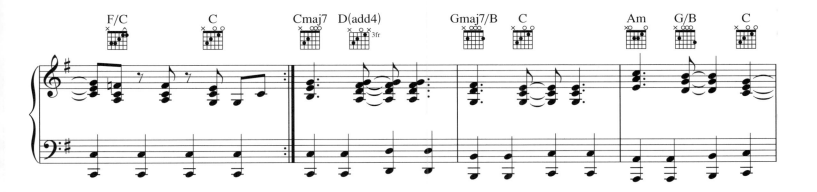

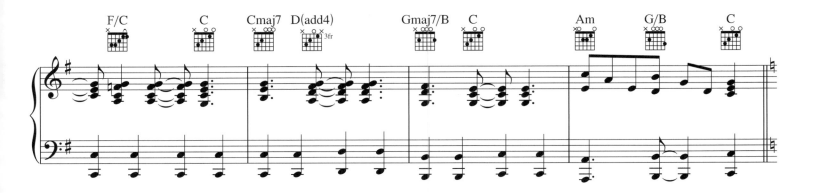

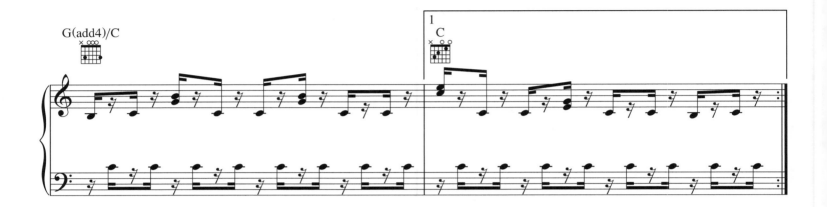

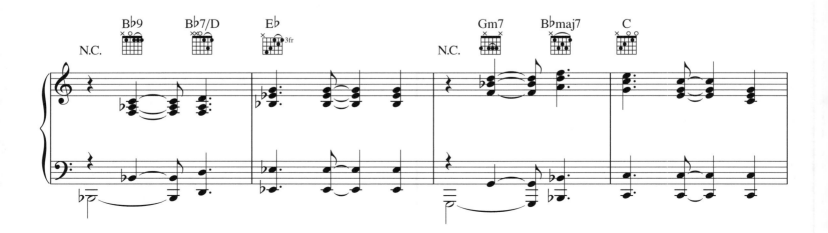

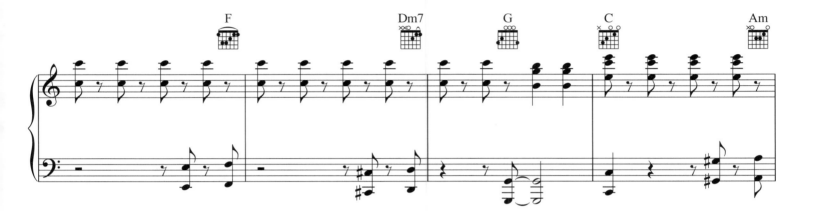

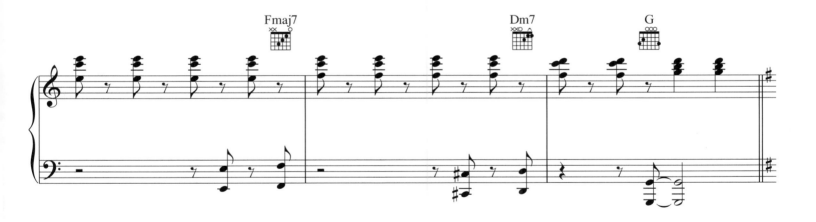

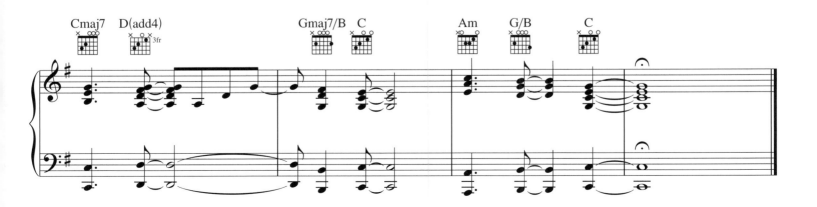

I'VE LOVED THESE DAYS

Words and Music by
BILLY JOEL

oh we can on-ly go___ so far___ on cav-i-ar___

and cab-er-net.___

(End instrumental)

We drown our doubts___ in dry cham-pagne___ and soothe our souls___
So be-fore we end___ and then be-gin___ we'll drink a toast___

with fine co-caine.___ I don't know why___ I e-ven care,___
to how it's been.___ A few more hours___ to be com-plete,___

we'll get so high _____ and get _____ no - where. _____ We'll have to change _
a few more nights _____ on sat - in sheets. _____ A few more times _

_____ our jad - ed ways _____
_____ that I can say _____

but I've loved these _____

I've loved these _____ days. _____

Roz Levin

MIAMI 2017
(Seen the Lights Go Out on Broadway)

Words and Music by
BILLY JOEL

Moderately, with a half time feel

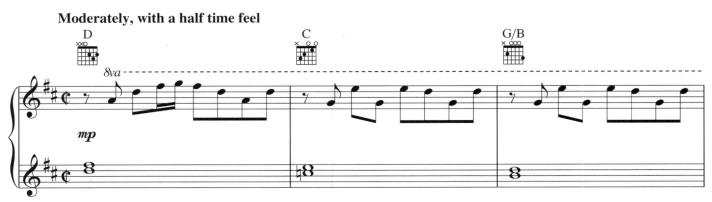

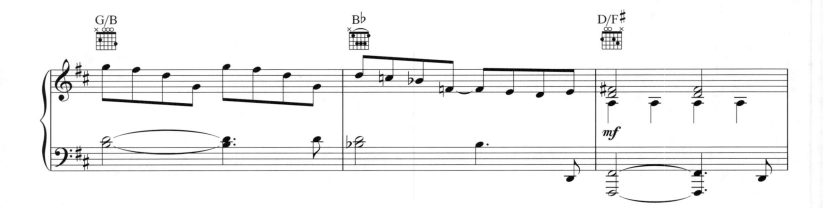

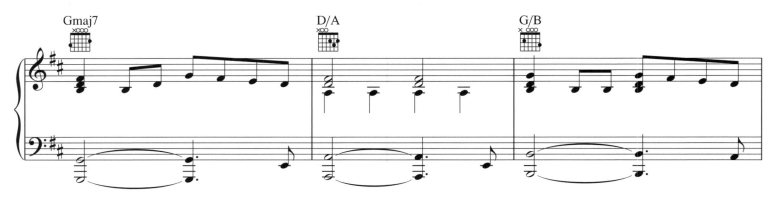

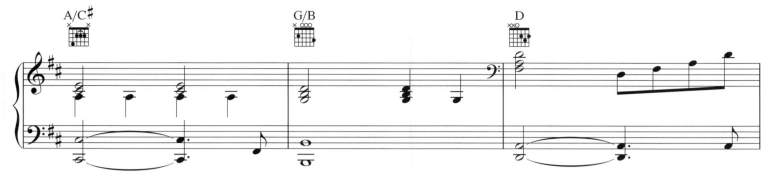

And life went on ____ be - yond ___ the Pal - i - sades,

they all bought Cad - il - lacs, ___ and left there

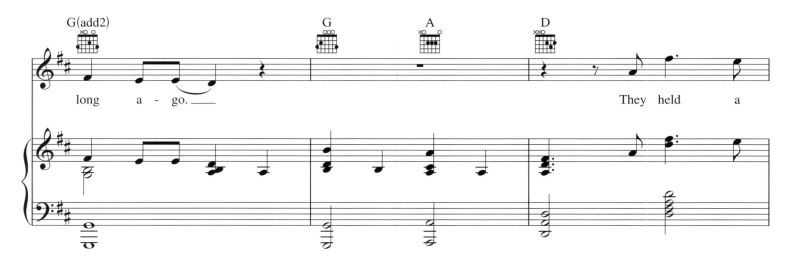

long a - go. ___ They held a

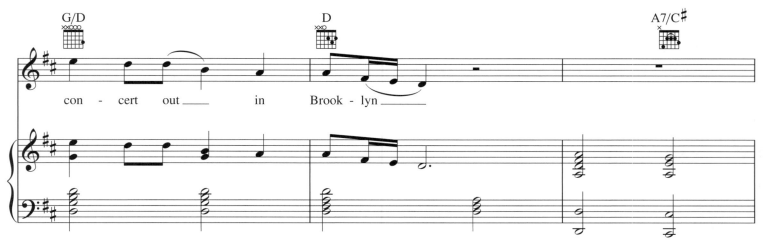

con - cert out ___ in Brook - lyn _____

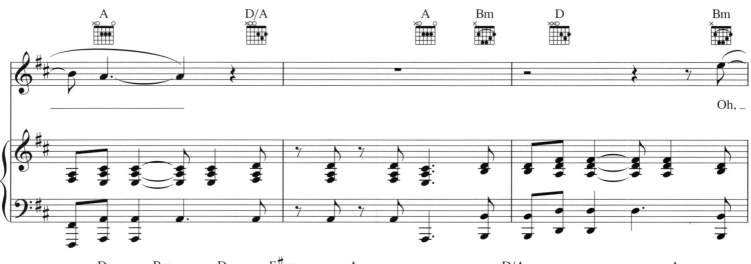

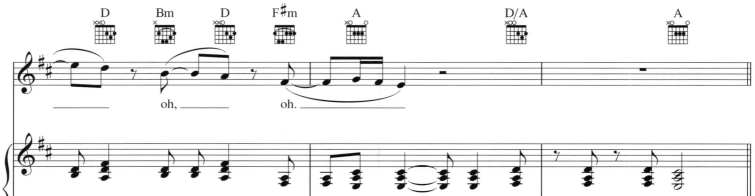

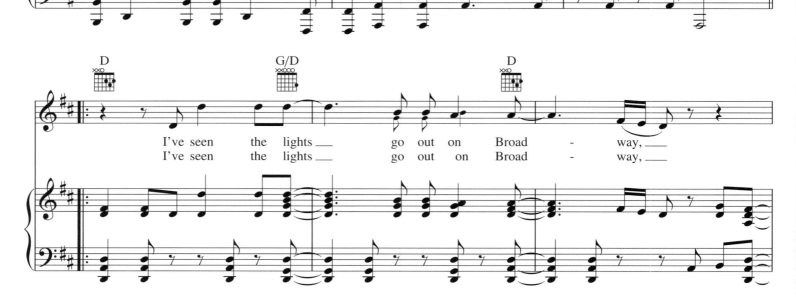

You know we al-
The boats were wait-

- most did-n't no - tice it. We'd seen it all
- ing at the bat - ter - y the un - ion

___ the time ___ on For - ty - Sec - ond Street. ___
went on strike; they nev-er sailed ___ at all. ___

They burned the church - es up ___ in Har -
They sent a car - rier out ___ from Nor -

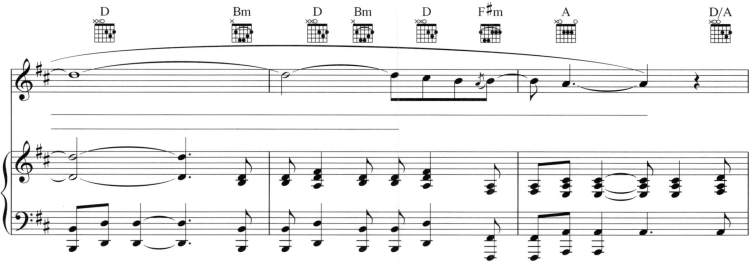

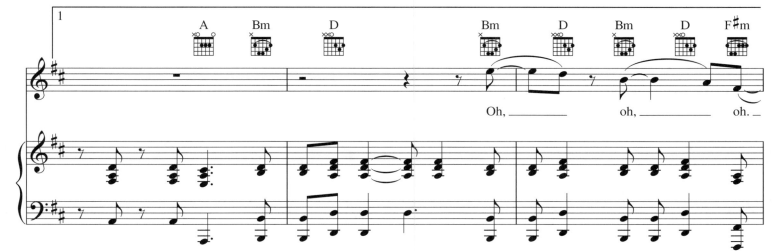

Oh, _____ oh, _____ oh. __

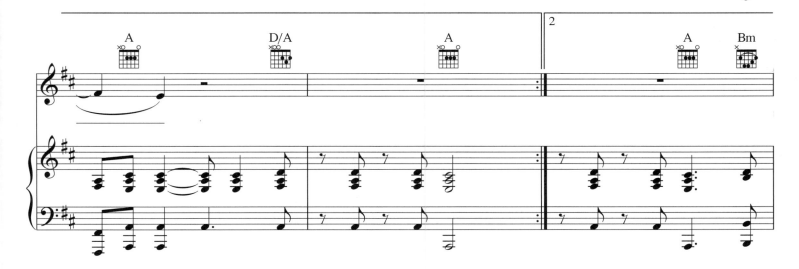

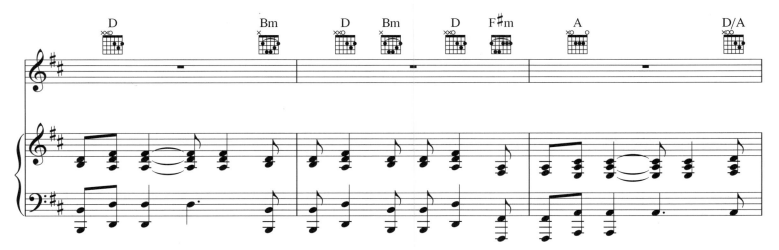

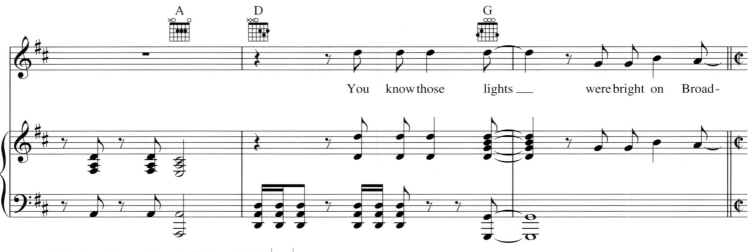

You know those lights ___ were bright on Broad-

Moderately, with a half time feel (♩ = ♩)

- way, ___ that was so

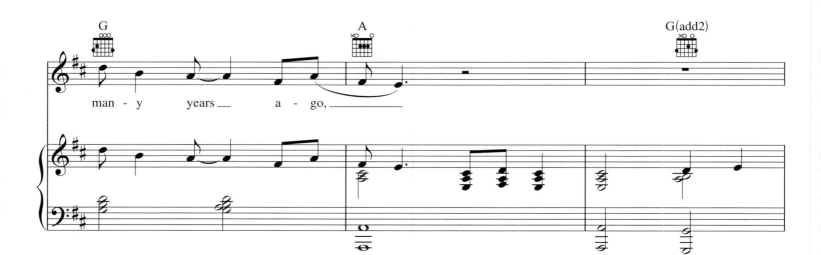

man - y years ___ a - go, ___

be - fore we all ___ lived here in Flo - ri - da,

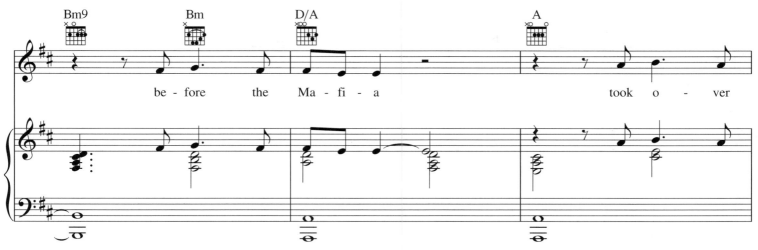

be - fore the Ma - fi - a took o - ver

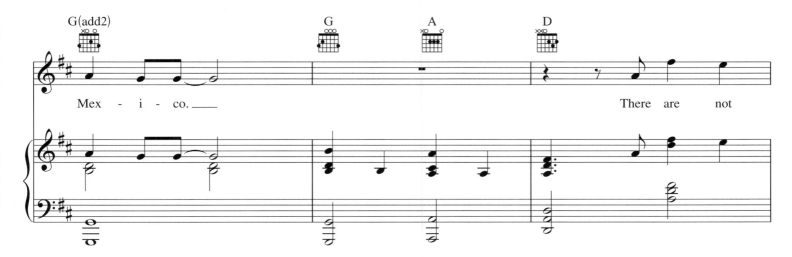

Mex - i - co. _____ There are not

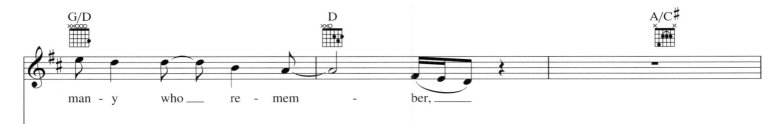

man - y who ___ re - mem - ber, _____

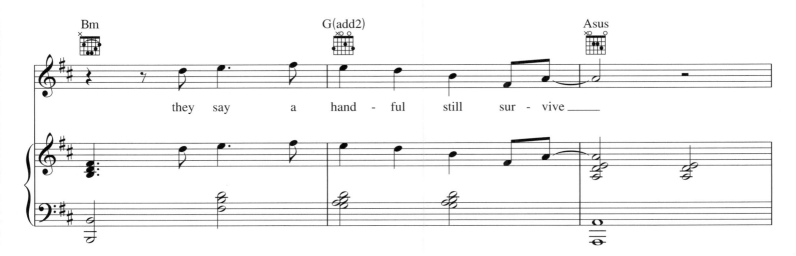

they say a hand - ful still sur - vive _____

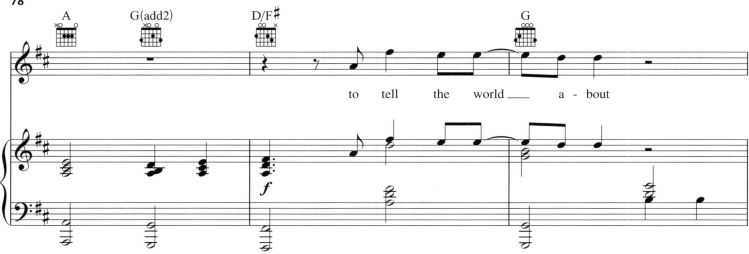

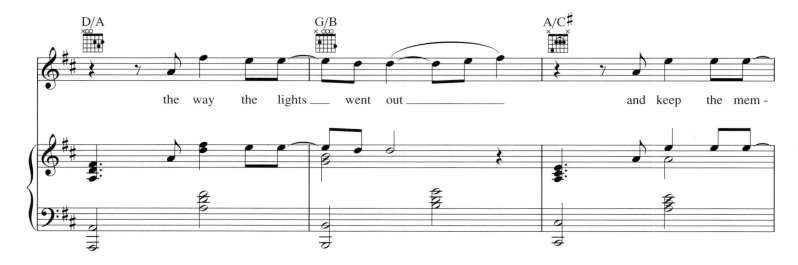

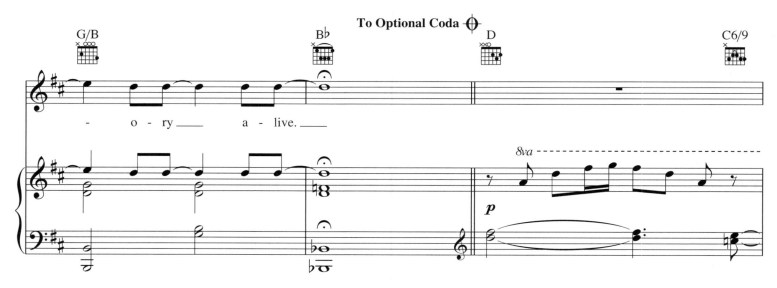

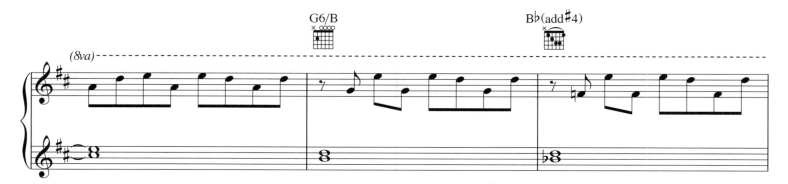

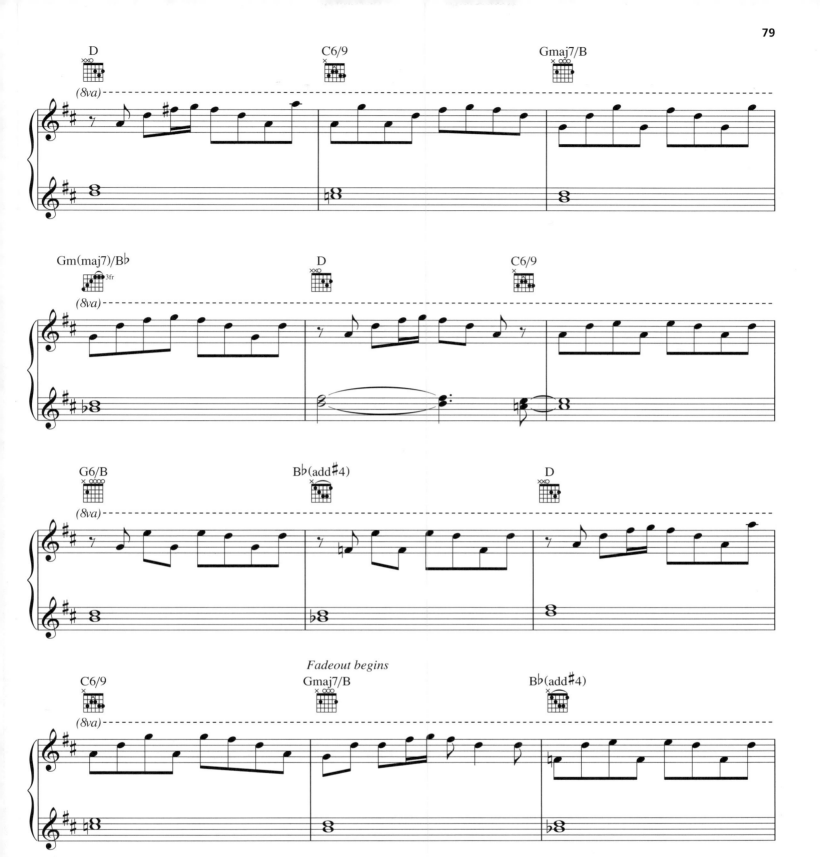

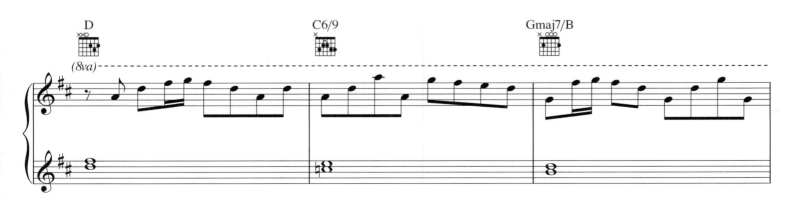

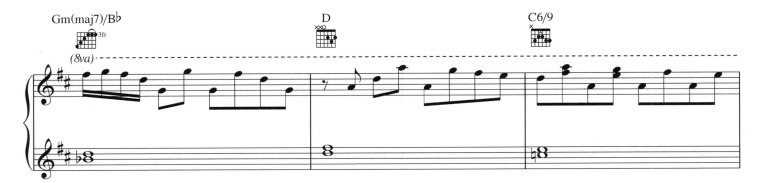

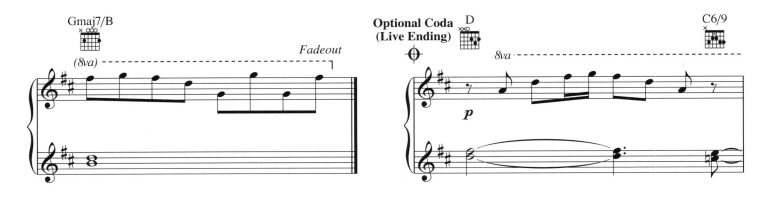

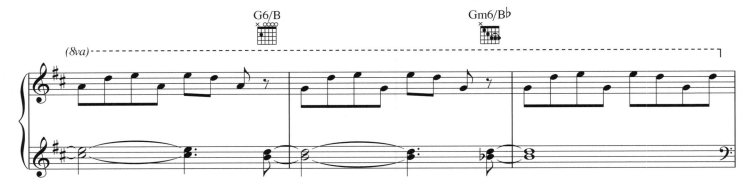

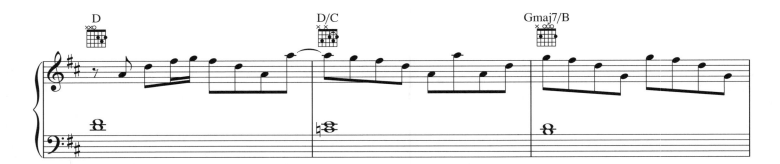

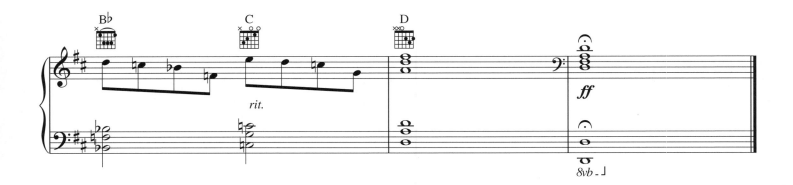